Your Step-by-Step Guide to Building Wealth:

# Why Invest

Understanding the Power of Growth

Dennis Watts

# Contents

Your Step-by-Step Guide to Building Wealth: ................................................................. 2
Why Invest? ................................................................................................................... 2
From Paycheck to Powerhouse: The Allure of Investing. .............................................. 3
Here are some compelling reasons to embark on your investment adventure. ............ 4
The Power of Time: Starting Early is Key ..................................................................... 6
Understanding Your Investment Goals: The Roadmap to Success .............................. 7
Risk and Reward: Balancing the Scales ....................................................................... 8
Building a Diversified Portfolio: Spreading Your Wings ................................................ 9
Building a Diversified Portfolio: Spreading Your Wings .............................................. 11
Common Investment Myths Debunked ....................................................................... 13
Getting Started Resources .......................................................................................... 14
Taking Action: Putting Your Investment Knowledge into Practice. ............................. 15
Investing for the Future: Embracing a Long-Term Mindset. ....................................... 17
Building a Secure and Prosperous Future .................................................................. 18
Disclaimer .................................................................................................................... 19

# Your Step-by-Step Guide to Building Wealth:

# Why Invest?
1. Understanding the Power of Growth!
2. Welcome to the Wonderful World of Investing!

You are taking the first step towards building a secure and prosperous future! This book serves as your initial guidepost on the exciting journey of investing. We'll explore why investing is crucial for achieving your financial goals and the power of compound interest, your greatest ally in wealth creation.

# From Paycheck to Powerhouse: The Allure of Investing.

Have you ever wondered how the wealthy accumulate vast amounts of money? While inheritance and luck might play a role for a small number, investing is the primary engine of wealth creation for most successful individuals.

Investing is allocating your money towards various assets with the expectation of generating income or profit over time. Imagine planting a seed: with proper care, it grows into a vigorous plant, bearing fruit season after season. Similarly, investing allows your money to "grow," yielding returns that can significantly increase your financial well-being.

Here are some compelling reasons to embark on your investment adventure.

**Outpace Inflation:** Inflation, the gradual rise in prices over time, erodes the purchasing power of money. A simple example: a loaf of bread that costs $3 today might cost $3.50 in a few years. Investing allows money to grow faster than inflation, allowing you to maintain and potentially increase your purchasing power.

**Achieve Financial Goals:** Do you dream of owning a home, providing for your children's education, or retiring comfortably? Investing helps you turn these aspirations into reality. By strategically investing based on your specific goals, you can amass the funds needed to achieve your goals.

**Compound Interest:** It's the concept of earning interest on your initial investment and the earned interest from previous periods. This creates a snowball effect, where your money grows exponentially over time. Let's illustrate the power of compound interest with a simple example: Imagine you invest $1,000 for two year at an annual interest rate of 5%. After one year, you'll earn $50 in interest, bringing your total to $1,050. In year two, you'll earn interest not just on the original $1,000 but also on the $50 you earned previously. So, you'll receive $52.50 in interest, bringing your total to $1,102.50. As you continue investing and the years go by, the snowball effect takes hold, significantly increasing your wealth.

# The Power of Time: Starting Early is Key

The best way to maximize the benefits of compound interest is to start saving early. The longer your money has time to grow, the more potent the compounding effect becomes. Consider this: If you start investing $1,000 annually at a 7% interest rate at age 25 and continue saving until you retire at age 65, your total investment contribution would be $40,000. However, thanks to annual compound interest, the value of your investment could grow to a staggering $199,635!

If you wait until 40 to begin investing the same amount at the same rate, your total investment contribution would be $25,000 by retirement. However, due to the shorter timeframe, annual compound interest has less time to work its magic, resulting in a significantly lower total of $63,249. This example highlights the stark difference starting early can make. The sooner you start investing, the more time your money has to grow exponentially through compound interest.

# Understanding Your Investment Goals: The Roadmap to Success

Investing is not a one-size-fits-all endeavor. Defining your specific financial goals before delving into the investment landscape is crucial.
**Consider the following questions:**

**What are your short-term goals?**
Are you saving for a house down payment, a dream vacation, or a new car? These goals typically have a shorter time horizon (less than five years) and might require a more secure or very conservative investment approach.

**What are your long-term goals?** Do you aspire to a comfortable retirement, funding your children's education, or leaving a legacy? These goals have a longer time horizon (over five years) and can benefit from a more growth-oriented investment strategy. Once you understand your goals and their timeframes, you can tailor your investment strategy accordingly. This involves determining your risk tolerance - your comfort level with potential investment losses.

# Risk and Reward: Balancing the Scales

Every investment carries some degree of risk. The risk level is associated with the potential for both gains and losses. Higher-risk investments generally offer higher returns but have a greater chance of experiencing losses. Lower-risk investments typically offer lower returns but provide more stability and some chance of experiencing losses.

## Understanding Your Risk Tolerance
Risk tolerance is assessing how comfortable you are with potential losses. There are several factors can influence your risk tolerance, including:

**Age:** Generally, younger investors have a longer time horizon and can, therefore, tolerate more risk. As retirement draws closer, risk tolerance might decrease or change as you prioritize preserving your capital.

**Financial Goals:** The timeframe associated with your goals plays a role. Short-term goals require a more secure or very conservative approach, while long-term goals can benefit from a strategy incorporating some risk.

**Financial Situation:** Your overall financial stability can influence your risk tolerance. A secure emergency fund and minimal debt make you more comfortable with potentially volatile investments.

# Building a Diversified Portfolio: Spreading Your Wings

You can create a diversified investment portfolio once you understand your desired risk tolerance. Diversification is the fundamental principle of mitigating risk by spreading investments across different asset classes. These asset classes have varying risk-return profiles, and their performance can be independent. Here are some of the main asset classes:

**Stocks:** Represent ownership in a company. Stock can offer the potential for high returns on investments through capital appreciation (stock price increase) and dividend payouts (a share of the company's profits). However, stocks also carry the risk of price fluctuations and potential losses.

**Bonds:** These are essentially loans between parties. They offer a fixed income stream (interest payments) and are considered less risky than stocks. However, bond prices can also fluctuate, and their returns are typically low.

**Cash Equivalents:** These include money market accounts and certificates of deposit (CDs). They offer a low level of risk and a guaranteed return but also the lowest potential for growth over time.

**Real Estate:** Investing in rental properties and real estate investment trusts can offer steady income and potential for capital appreciation. However, real estate is a less liquid asset with higher upfront costs and ongoing management requirements. However, real estate investing also carries the risk of price fluctuations and potential losses.

# Building a Diversified Portfolio: Spreading Your Wings

We've discussed the importance of diversification in mitigating risk. Let's delve deeper into some of the standard investment vehicles you can utilize to build a diversified portfolio:

**Mutual Funds:** Mutual Funds are manage professionally by portfolio managers that invest in various assets, such as stocks, bonds, or other asset classes. They offer diversification, professional management, and lower investment minimums than buying individual stocks or bonds.

**Exchange-Traded Funds (ETFs):** Like mutual funds, ETFs are baskets of securities traded on stock exchanges like individual stocks. They offer diversification, low expense ratios (management fees), and intraday trading flexibility.

**Individual Stocks:** Owning shares in specific companies allows you to benefit from their growth and dividend payouts. However, investing in individual stocks requires more research and carries a higher risk profile than diversified funds.

**Bonds:** Government and corporate bonds offer a fixed income stream and are considered less risky than stocks.

However, bond prices fluctuate, and their returns are typically lower. For diversification, you can invest in bond funds.

**Real Estate:** Investing in real estate or REITs can provide steady income and capital appreciation potential. However, real estate requires significant capital and ongoing management and is a less liquid asset compared to stocks or bonds.

**The Role of Financial Advisors:** While this book empowers individuals to become knowledgeable about investing, it also acknowledges the potential benefits of seeking professional guidance from a qualified financial advisor, particularly for complex financial situations. Here are some instances where a financial advisor's expertise can be valuable:

**Complex Financial Situations:** If you have a high net worth, complex financial goals, or limited investment knowledge, a financial advisor can provide personalized guidance and navigate more intricate investment options.

**Retirement Planning:** Planning for retirement is important, and a financial advisor can help design a customized strategy considering your income, expenses, and desired retirement lifestyle.

**Estate Planning:** Financial advisors can guide estate planning strategies, such as trusts and life insurance, to ensure assets are distributed according to wishes.

# Common Investment Myths Debunked

Many misconceptions surround investing, deterring people from taking the first step. Here are some common myths debunked:

**Myth 1:** You will need a large amount of Money to Start Investing: You don't need a hefty sum to begin your investment journey. Many investment options, like low-minimum mutual funds, allow you to start small and gradually increase your contributions over time.

**Myth 2:** The Stock Market is Risky: While inherent risk exists, investing over a long-term horizon can allow you to ride out market fluctuations and benefit from potential growth. Diversification across various asset classes further mitigates risk.

**Myth 3:** Investing is Complicated and Requires Expertise: With readily available educational resources and user-friendly investment platforms, starting your investment journey can be more straightforward.

## Getting Started Resources

The world of investing offers a wealth of resources to equip you for success. Here are some helpful starting points for your investment journey:

**Investment Books and Articles:** Numerous publications and online resources offer insights into various investment strategies, asset classes, and market trends.
**Financial Podcasts and Videos:** Educational podcasts and videos can provide a more engaging and digestible way to learn about investing concepts.
Consulting these resources and familiarizing yourself with the fundamentals may help you build a strong foundation for navigating the exciting investing world.

# Taking Action: Putting Your Investment Knowledge into Practice.

Understanding investing concepts is crucial, but the real power lies in taking action and putting your knowledge into practice. Here are some practical steps to initiate your investment journey:

**Assess Your Financial Health:** Before investing, thoroughly assess your current financial situation. This includes calculating your net worth (assets minus liabilities), creating a budget to track income and expenses, and identifying outstanding debts.

**Set Your Investment Goals:** As discussed earlier, defining your goals is fundamental. Are you saving for a down payment on a house in five years, a child's college education in 15 years, or a comfortable retirement 30 years later? Setting clear and realistic goals will guide your investment strategy.

**Evaluate Your Risk Tolerance:** Honesty about your comfort level with potential losses is crucial. Consider your age, financial goals, and overall risk aversion to determine your risk tolerance.

**Research Investment Options:** Now that you understand your goals and risk tolerance, explore various investment options. Research different asset classes and their associated investment, such as mutual funds, ETFs, and individual securities.

**Develop an Investment Strategy:** Based on your research and risk tolerance, formulate a diversified investment strategy that allocates your capital across different asset classes. Consider using online tools and consult with a financial advisor and resources to help you build a suitable portfolio.

**Invest Consistently:** Regardless of the amount, establish a habit of investing regularly. This can be a fixed sum monthly or a percentage of your income. Remember, patience and consistency are essential to long-term investment success.

**Monitor and Rebalance Your Portfolio:** Markets are dynamic, and your investment needs might evolve. Monitoring your portfolio's performance and rebalancing it periodically may help maintain a desired asset allocation and risk profile.

**Investing for the Future: Embracing a Long-Term Mindset.**

Investing is a marathon, not a sprint. The key to building wealth is to cultivate a long-term perspective. Avoid the temptation of short-term market fluctuations and emotional decisions. By remaining disciplined and focused on your long-term goals, you can weather market ups and downs and experience the power of compound interest.

**Building a Secure and Prosperous Future**

Investing equips you to take control of your financial future, achieve your goals, and create a legacy for yourself and your loved ones. The journey to financial security is a continuous learning process. Embrace the learning curve, adapt your strategies as needed, and stay committed to all your financial goals. By understanding the power of compound interest, crafting a sound investment plan, and exercising discipline, you can unlock economic opportunities and embark on a secure and prosperous future.

## Disclaimer

Each person's finances are different, and they should seek independent financial advice from a professional. Therefore, the book information does not serve as financial advice and should not be relied upon to be accurate and complete.

Money is a topic that many people find intimidating or overwhelming. However, mastering your money can lead to financial freedom and a more comfortable life. You can take several steps to master your money, including setting financial goals, creating a budget, managing debt, and investing wisely. This book explore these steps and provides tips and resources to help you master your money.

Blank

Blank

Blank

Blank

Blank

Blank

Blank

Blank

27

Blank

Blank

Blank

Blank

32

33

www.ingramcontent.com/pod-product-compliance
Lightning Source LLC
Chambersburg PA
CBHW070958220526
45471CB00007B/3077